This is my second book of poetry,
and like my first, is a collection of random poems,
written mostly over the last ten years,
though some are older.

The poems are once again separated
into sections, -
'Family'- 'Hull' - 'Remembrance'- 'Time' - 'Aging'
and 'Nature' though some could fall into more than
one section, given their subject matter.

I hope you enjoy reading the poems
as much as I enjoyed writing them,
thank you for your interest.

John Fairclough

This book is dedicated to my two grandsons
Joe and Sam,
with my thanks for all they have done for me.

Special thanks again to my wife Maureen and my
daughter Nicole for their help and encouragement.

To my friend Phil Corby for his good work
to Monty and all my friends at the Muse.

And once again to the people who applaud
when I stand up and read my poems -

My thanks to you all.

Cover: Original Oil Painting by John Fairclough

The author asserts the moral right under the copyright, designs and
patents act 1988 to be identified as the author of this work.
Copyright John Fairclough 2023

ISBN 978-1-9161028-7-3

Design and artwork by Phil Corby
Printed by Fisk Printers Hull

Contents

Family

Hull

Rememberance

Time

Contents

Nature

Ageing

Family

The following poems are about 'family' - some about particular members of my family, some about particular events within my family, - old, young, happy, sad or just random events, but all of them with particular meaning for me.

Future Hope

They're my boys,
I'm with them almost every day,
and, truth to say, I cannot imagine
my life without them,
and I like to think they feel the same about me,
although now I can already see
that these halcyon days cannot go on for ever,
and the books that we read, and the games that we play,
and the bike rides on warm summer days . . . .

They're my boys,
and they have all their lives ahead,
and though I often dread what the future forebodes,
as they make their ways down life's many roads,
I can only hope that on some 'future day'
They'll smile, recalling, and laughingly say,
"Remember when grandpa . . . . "

20th April 2000

Hope Fulfilled

They were my boys back then, now they are grown men,
grown up and grown out,
back then I never imagined my life without them in it every day,
but, here today they have moved away, they have partners, careers,
houses of their own, and aspirations which I have never known.
And yet, though twenty three years have now flown away,
since I wrote 'Future hope', and that once 'future day' is now almost
here,
But I have no fear, my hopes for them have been fulfilled,
for they phone, and visit, and we laugh a lot together,
they are my grandsons, life is good, and I am content.

20th April 2023

The two poems, 'Future Hope' and 'Hope Fulfilled' were both written about
my grandsons, Joe and Sam, and though written twenty three years apart,
and they are now both grown men, the sentiments are the same.

They are still 'My boys'

Just a Book

Reading the last page I found myself
almost weeping,
not wanting it to end,
and thinking to myself that men don't cry,
and wondering why
this one had effected me so much.

It was just a book,
just words arranged and printed
on a blank white page,
and yet they filled me with such rage,
such passion and such pity,
that they moved me close to tears.

And reading the last few
paragraphs once more,
My thoughts turned to my mum and dad,
and the turbulent, troubled, traumatic,
life which they shared together,
and how their children still grieved for them.

After reading 'The amateur Marriage' by Anne Tyler.

The Old Lady

She's very old, and very frail,
her colour now a whitewash pale,
her movements soft and creaky slow,
her hair a whispy grey-white snow,
her memory now is not the same
sometimes she can't recall your name,
or what happened yesterday,
or what she was about to say.
Sometimes she doesn't even know you've been,
and questions, "Why, I haven't seen
our John in weeks, and he's forgot to
bring my sweets, and no-one ever comes
here anymore."

She's very old, and very grey,
her family grown up and gone away,
she lives alone, all by herself,
her husbands picture on the mantelshelf.
she has her tele, and her friends,
and sometimes, on the nice weekends,
she stays over at her daughters house,
and complains, her lined face so sad,
"Our Johns so much like his dad,
he never remembers anything,
and now he's forgotten my sweets again."

Continued

She's very old, but button bright,
and when I went round the other night
she seemed so glad to see me.
We chattered and talked of family and friends,
and then towards the very end,
as I was getting up to go, she said,
her voice so gentle slow,
"Thank you for the sweets our John,
I was practically down to the very last one.

She's very old, and next week she'll complain
that I haven't been round to see her again,
"I haven't seen anyone since last Monday,
and I've not seen our John in a month of Sundays"
but she's always so glad to see my face,
though often I feel that I'm in disgrace,
she's old, my mother, and getting slow,
but she needs me, and I love her so.

Painted Wooden Apples

Painted wooden apples, hung up on a string,
such a simple gift, which you know will always bring
a smile to her face, as, given pride of place,
she hangs them on the hallway wall, and you recall,
in the place where you hide your emotions,
that feeling of joy at her smile.

Just like all the pictures she displays on her walls,
oils and watercolours, which she always calls
'Dad's collection', but I know, and she knows,
though neither will say, that she never would
part with them, come what may, and you recall,
in the place where you hide all your pride,
that feeling of joy at her words.

And the comments she will often make
when she reads all the things which I write,
and the care which she always takes
to ensure that they sound just right,
and her criticism is truthful but always mild,
for she handles my poetry just like a child,
with warmth, and feeling, and loving care,
and watching her, you know,
in the place where you hide all your love,
that feeling of joy which only a daughter can give.

Angels II

They are still there, up in the roof beams,
so it seems, they must be real,
I can feel it, in my heart
and in my bones,
that this is something more
than just medical science.

Across the room she smiles questioningly,
not knowing my thoughts,
and wondering at my sudden attention,
but I have no intention of enlightening her
as to my mind's wonderings,
I hear the beating of celestial wings
within my head, -
She is not gone, against all odds she carries on,
and through her my own life continues.

And the Christmas angels still always say,
in my stilted and somewhat prosaic way,
"Someone to watch over you"
for I believe that they still do,
and keep my faith that they always will.

29th June, 2010.

*In 1993 my wife was told she had breast cancer, and would need a
mastectomy to effect a cure, since then she has had a continuous
battle with the disease, (including further operations) and is still
on a medical regime to control it.*
*Since that time, at Christmas, I have always sent her a small
ceramic angel as one of her presents, with the message,*
"Someone to watch over you"

You Are (Perfect Day)

You are the flower that brightens my May,
the perfect in my perfect day,
You are the rock that makes me roll,
the guardian angel protecting my soul,
You are the high that makes my noon.
the remembering of that lovely tune,
You are the grand in my canyon deep,
the gee that keeps my whiz from sleep,
You are the jelly jumping in my bean,
the finest hop my scotch has seen,
And from the charm that's in my lucky,
to the fortune in my fortune cookie.
From the pow that's in my wow!
you really ought to know by now,
that I want you to forever stay. . .

The perfect in my perfect day.

Birthday Girl

She sits, bewildered, in the midst of it all,
thinking of times she alone can recall,
times where her memories are lingering yet,
times of delight, and times of regret.
Her children around her are a babble of sound,
with their childrens photographs passing around,
and everyone's smiling, each having their say,
and snaps in the garden, recording the day.

And her gift is presented, and all are agreed,
that as presents go this is just what she'll need,
and she smiles, then she cries, with her eyes far away,
and she blows out her candles, recalling the day
when her children were children, and the future unknown,
and she wonders again at how the times flown . . .

Trustees

We are only trustees
for those that come after us,
our children, and our
children's children.
And each generation must play
it's part, and pass on, with head,
and hand, and heart,
must pass on our hopes, pass on
our dreams, pass on our courage,
and everything which seems
to make this life worthwhile.
For everything which we hold dear,
we hold in trust for them,
for they are our children,
and our children's children.

Mother and Son

They sit together, on the steps of that sunlit square,
with the late afternoon sun dappling the warm stones,
and Spain, on a lazy, late September day,
becomes a magical, mythical place,
the Alhambra Palace is all around us, its buildings,
the minarets, the fountains, the sheer splendor of it all,
almost takes your breath away, - yet leaves you
with a sense of calm which goes to your very soul,
and I sense that they can feel the magic.

I am an old man now, living mostly on memories,
and though I know that we are all only trustees,
to our children, and our children's children,
I sit there quietly, hoping that I have done enough,
that I have filled their minds with all the stuff
of wonder and imagination.
And as I watch my daughter and grandson sitting there,
I offer up a silent prayer, hoping that they too,
can feel the wonder of this magical, mythical, place.

Set to Fly

They're growing up so quickly now,
"Oh grandpa." they say, in mock dismay,
when I fail to keep up to speed
on the football computer game,
or cannot even remember the name
of the latest pop group,
"Oh grandpa." they say, as they turn away,
their fingers flying over the computer keys,
the darting mouse under their hand,
bright images changing at their command.

They'e growing up so quickly now,
and I cannot keep pace with their restless energy,
and now it often seems to me,
that maybe I am losing them,
that maybe the days of miracle and wonder
are over and through,
and there is nothing that I can say or do
to try and bring them back.

They're growing up so quickly now,
and I can feel them set to fly -
and yet as days and weeks run by,
sometimes, from a clear blue sky,
something happens,- maybe its just a hand,
confidently placed in mine, or a telephone call,
a smile, a sign, - just some little thing that lets me know,
that though they may be set to go,
I will not be abandoned or forgotten.

HULL

Riding pastures, vaulted sky,
Soothes the restless inner eye
My land, my homeland.

All the poems in this collection have connections to Hull,
either directly, through history or heritage, or indirectly
through association or tradition.
Most of them are recollections, memories, stories, or just feelings,
which I have gathered from a lifetime of living and working
in or around Hull.
It is my home town, a place of which I will always be proud.

Under The Big Sky

Maybe it has to do with reputation, or maybe,
to a lesser extent, location, though much
of it stems from our streak of independence,
that resonance of living on the edge,
that willingness of us all to pledge
our allegiance to this isolated city.

But call it what you will, it is there still,
this pride of place, this sense of being
more than just another northern city.
more than just 'somewhere up north'.
Even though this city has a less than
pleasing image in the eyes of the nation.

More, I think, the creation of prejudice
then any reasoned thought, but now sadly caught
within the nations consciousness,
and accepted as truth, - more or less,
just a part of the great North/South divide
where often honesty is pushed aside.

So maybe it has more to do with conception,
the endless images of fish docks, and back to back
houses row upon row, and no one ever gets to know
about Queens gardens, the Ferens, or the Deep,
so 'The land of green ginger' is still ours to keep,
under the big sky, living on the edge.

Homeland

So far away, and yet so familiar,
there seemed to be an echo, a resonance
of history and of home, as if somehow
I'd always known these places,
their names falling familiar on my ears,
the years of history opening up before my eyes,
each building, each village and town
seemed to be gently pulling me down
unknown, yet familiar, roads.

Was it imagined, was it only vaguely remembered dreams,
or unrealised schemes, that made me feel that I'd been
here before, or maybe was it something more,
that my own country's history was mirrored here,
for as my stay lengthened it all seemed so clear,
as I walked through the leaves of gold and brown,
watching the trees shed their autumn gown
as they climbed the hill, that feeling still,
of being in this place before, of seeing more
than just the surface reality, there always, somehow,
seemed to be a different dimension.

And as I walked the covered bridges,
past the white and pristine country church,
I felt my heart begin to search,
as the echoes reverberated back through my mind,
and once again I began to find that easy familiarity
as names like York and Beverley began to appear
on the crossroads signs.
And I had to smile to myself as I remembered
the American saying about this place -
"This is not reality, this is New Hampshire!"
or the old east riding, I thought to myself
as I turned down the road marked simply 'to Hull'
and began to head for home.

Turning Days

The colours are changing, and slanted light
beckons the eye, and fills the vaulted sky
with wonderments of restless clouds.
Out on the river, the surface changing,
currents swiftly re-arranging the tidal flow,
and muddy banks you've come to know
change shape and slide away as sandbars shift,
and on the turning of the day,
you feel the movement.

Trees march the hill, their colours ever changing,
never still, the wind commanding leaf and limb,
as morning mist makes ghostly dim the landscape.
And the earth turns, green gives way to gold and brown,
and deeper down, beside the pond,
the reeds are shedding their feathered heads,
preparing again their winter beds,
and on the turning of the day,
you feel the movement.

The light is changing, moving still, cloud shadow patterns
climb the hill, changing its shape and substance,
the land huddles down against the wind's increasing edge,
each field and furrow, ridge and ledge, draws in upon itself.
And the earth turns, as winter chills invade
the hill, and frost permeates the stony ground,
and all around you see the change in natures way,
and on the turning of the day,
you feel again the movement.

The Unemployed

"No job today" the timekeeper said, as they turned him from the gate,
"No job today" they echoed, as they left him to his fate,
and the streets were dark and shiny grey, and the rain
was a steady drizzle, and he knew before he'd even asked,
there would be no job today - for he was the unemployed.

His hopes had been so high that day he'd walked out of the school,
Two "A's" six "O's." his tutor said, "They'll see you're no-ones fool"
but now he knew just what they thought, he saw it in their eyes,
they said "No job today" as they turned him away,
and he knew that they despised - the unemployed.

For three long years how hard he tried, he queued for interviews,
he lied, he pleaded, begged, broke down and cried,
but still the stony voice replied, "No jobs today'
And each time that he was turned away his black despair would grow
As he felt the stigma of his life, he was - the unemployed.

And as he walked the streets, past the bright lit stores,
despite himself, sometimes he would pause,
and stare at the things he could never afford to buy,
and he felt such anger, such despair, that no-one
ever seemed to care about - the unemployed.

And the note which he left his parents read,
that he was sorry for bringing this shame on their head,
but he just could not face another long day,
of constantly being turned away, he just couldn't face
another day on the dole, another day with despair
destroying his soul, he just couldn't face another
long day of being - the unemployed.

In the 'Hull Daily Mail' the headline read "Young man hangs himself after three years of being unemployed."

Kids

When I was a kid one of my friends had
a big orange rubber dingy(war surplus)
which we used to sail in the local drain,
and when you moved about it was a bit
like walking on a balloon.
And we would all lean over the edge and paddle,
and the big orange dingy would go round and round
like a Catherine wheel, getting no-where.

When I was a kid we would go to 'logs' and play soldiers,
using sticks with bits of rag tied to them as flags,
we'd crawl and squirm under and between the massive
piles of timber, never even thinking about the danger,
and go home with our trousers torn and our knees cut.

When I was a kid we had a contest to see who was the bravest
at walking along the parapets of the drain bridges,
and who was the last one to start running when the 'parky' came,
when I was a kid we would walk all the way to 'castle hill'
(which was about a hundred miles away in our imaginations!)
and we all learnt to swim in a place called 'sandy bottom'
and games of 'reallioh' lasted all night, and summer lasted forever!

When I was a kid we roasted potatoes in the embers of bonfire night,

And went 'knocking up ginger' - and 'chudding' in Sutton,

And life was so simple . . . . when I was a kid!

Say a Little Prayer

If the day ever comes when Hull City are top
of the first division, with three points to spare,
or when Arthur Scargill stops using derision,
and really shows some kind of care,
when Hull Brewary ales start tasting good,
when MFI furniture really is made of wood,
then the day has arrived when maybe we should
start to say a little prayer.

If the day ever comes when there is no vandalism
on Bransholme Estate, or when British Rail trains
stop running late, when they stop making bombs,
and start making sense, when using your brain
is not an offence, when Sheffield has it's first flood,
then maybe its time we all should,
start to say a little prayer.

If the day ever comes when summer is filled with blue sky,
or when Yorkshire declares UDI, when Ian Botham bowls
out Clive Lloyd, or when Maggie becomes unemployed,
when tolerance is fact, and not just another word,
when the dogs of war will never again be heard,
then maybe its time we should all be prepared,
to say a little prayer.

Spurn Point

A lonely place, strung out between the empty sky
and the restless, ever present sea, a place of seagulls,
solitude, and me, - alone,
Sat on the rough tan sand, feeling the tiny crystals move
between the fingers of my outstretched hand.
The sky a vault of cobalt blue, vast and empty,
It's colours forever changing hue as it drains away over the far horizon.

The sea seems huge and sullen, it's bands of colours
seem almost solid, azure, brown and silky green,
glazed by the sun's relentless sheen,
and far out to sea a band of the darkest blue
marks the place my eyes are always turning to.

There seems a silence everywhere, which holds me there
like a mighty hand, pinning me down to the glistening sand.
and yet, the sound of the surf is always there ,
pounding relentlessly against the old breakwaters,
which, battered and barnacle encrusted still stand,
a token of man's last glib defiance to the sea and to this alien land,
they stand, forlorn, festooned with seaweed,
Shells, and shreds of net, an empty gesture,
Lost against the sea's unending threat.

This strange and lonely alien strip of land,
this narrow wedge of reed flecked, hard edged sand,
where only seabirds swoop and soar,
where the only sound is the ceaseless roar
of the surf as it drives in relentlessly,
this place of seagulls, solitude, and me - alone.

It Should Have Been Rutherford

Don't get me wrong, I have nothing against Philip Larkin,
as a person or a poet, in fact I really liked his poetry,
it's just that, well, it seems to me,
that in a city of poets, and this is a city of poets,
maybe we could have found a 'native' one
to honour with a statue, - someone born here,
who grew up here,
someone who knew the sights, and the sounds,
and the very smell of the city.
Larkin wrote often about the city, - but he was never of the city,
he chose to work here, and he chose to stay,
but the line 'I was late getting away'
under his statue on Paragon Station,
hints at more than just speculation
about him to me, -
maybe it questioned where he really wanted to be?

But I know a poet who was born here, - on Albert Avenue,
and like me, - and maybe you, was raised here, and worked here,
and,- more importantly, - wrote his poetry here,
in and about the city, a 'native' if you like,
but I know his work would strike an instant resonance with anyone
who knows this city and it's people,
he is a simple poet, writing simple verse,
but he is a master of his craft,
he writes of ordinary, everyday subjects
which seem to take on extraordinary resonance
under the guidance of his practiced hand.
And all who read his words can understand,
and comprehend his meanings.
But would he appreciate a statue in Paragon Station?
he would probably smile, and ask only that the citation read,
'Hull's poet - Maurice Rutherford, - Hull born and bred'

Names

Hull Minster, the very sound of it is so strange,
with mechanical puddles all artistically arranged
to reflect the status of it's place and glorify it's name,
its appearance changed, - yet, somehow, still the same,
chic cafes, all with their chequered and stripy chairs
now form neat barriers around the squares,
and art and colour are everywhere
as the flood of tourists stop and stare.

The Proms have left London to visit here,
their music pervades our streets and pier -
as they play in the newly developed auditorium,
an outside setting for their recital,
as we all settle into our new found title,
Hull - City of Culture. 2017
once it was just our city, - a city without a cathedral,
but now it has culture, and a newly named Minster, -
and I'm so proud, and so glad, yet in a small way, somehow sad,
for to me, here inside, our church will forever be
our old, and much beloved, 'Holy Trinity'

A Northern City

I walked around all the installations,
already knowing the stories they were telling,
my heart swelling with pride as I saw
the colourful displays on the city's buildings,
this city where I had spent most of my life,
where I had lived through the strikes and the strife,
the bombed building playgrounds of my childhood years,
all the uncertainty, and all the fears, and the isolation,
the derision, of being that 'Northern city' whose name no-one knew.
And yet all my life that fierce pride of being a part of it,
of sharing that hard edged accent, of knowing full well
just what people meant when they spoke of hardship.
And now, suddenly, here it is, displayed for all the world to see,
This untold story of my city, - and of me!
I walked amongst the people of Hull on that night,
filled with pride at the sound and the sight,
of what we have achieved,
knowing that our unknown 'Northern City' had finally
gained it's long overdue recognition, it's coming of age.
and my heart raced as I gazed all around,
filled with the sight and the wonderful sound,
of a city proud of it's history, it's heritage,
and it's rightful sense of place.

Remembrance

Another set of remembrances, mostly my own,
as most are, though some have a more
universal theme or message.

It Should Have Been Raining

It should have been raining I thought,
as I stood there in the sunshine of a perfect
blue and white July day, watching,
as he was borne away upon the shoulders
of anonymous men.
I had not known him very well, the second
husband of a long time friend, but somehow
his untimely end had moved me more
than I cared to admit.

As I stood there, thinking of rain,
and feeling somehow guilty for my own life,
and it's continuing calm, watching,
as she walked by on her fathers arm,
her young life shattered once again,
and knowing nothing I could say, or do,
would help to ease her pain.

And I murmured condolences, briefly
touched hands, feeling inside I never would
understand the chance circumstances of our lives.
And as I walked slowly away through that
sun drenched, shadow dappled cemetery,
I felt unwanted anger rising in me, as I thought,
somehow bitterly, it should have been raining.

Echoes

And I can hear the echoes of the ghosts out of the past,
of the men of Mons and Marne who were shot,
and shelled, and gassed.
Who fought a war to end all wars, who fought to set us free,
who died in all their thousands for that hollow victory.

And I can hear the echoes of the men of Tripoli,
of Malaya and the Philippines and places strange to me,
who fought a war so bloody and now lie in an unmarked grave,
if they could see, would they applaud, the world they died to save ?

And I can hear the echoes of the soldiers of Vietnam,
who all knew the war they fought in was some politicians sham,
they were killed and they were wounded in a war they could not win,
and then shunned and left forgotten when they struggled home again.

And I dread to hear the echoes as on this mournful day,
the ships of troops and armour slide so fearsomely away,
they leave my country's pleasant land and head on out to sea,
they leave from Argentina too, to meet their destiny.

And dear God are we too blind to see what this is leading to,
that events are overtaking us, is there nothing we can do,
we must talk, and talk forever until reason has it's say,
for I dread to hear the echoes upon this mournful day.

Missing in November

A raw, grey November day,
and I sit on the rocks looking out
to the far reaches of the estuary,
watching the seagulls as, effortlessly,
they ride the gusting surge of the east wind,
swooping to pick and perch at the waters edge,
the smooth brown ledge of tidal bank.

The cutting edge of the wind bites against my cheek,
and I guess that, within a week, we may have
the first of winter's snow, for up along the estuary
I can already see the clouds piling high,
building up towards precipitation, and I think,
'Time to head for home' and standing,
I head on back, up the edge of the river,
watching as the squares of light appear in the houses
of the village, and already missing the glow
of the fireplace, and the welcoming warmth of her smile.

Pale Horseman

There's a pale horseman on my horizon
whose face I never see, he sits just beyond
the edge of vision, making judgement upon me,
I never see his features, and I never hear his voice,
but he appears in times of crisis when I know
I have a choice, between a good or bad thing,
a decision right or wrong,
and he sits in silent judgement,
never wanting to belong to all the thoughts inside my head,
all the worry and the doubt, but I can hear his scornful voice
rising in a silent shout, which echoes round
inside my head when I fall from his grace,
and I cannot live within myself,
                    for there is no hiding place.
and I know that throughout my life
                    I can never be set free,
the pale horseman of my conscience
                    will forever ride with me.

Dog Days

Dog days, each year they come, and who's to say,
who's hand will stay, or turn away
their all embracing symmetry.
In winter months, on greyclad days, they creep inside me,
like weevils, burrowing into heart and head,
and turning my half imagined dread into reality.
Dog days, when the slanting light is never quite right,
when time oppresses me and I can never seem to see
an ending, as the shifting, drifting indifferences of mankind,
like the tide out on the estuary, sweep over me, invisible,
leaving no scar, no hint of what the meanings are,
as sorrow stalks the slanting light,
and leaves no line of sound or sight
against the sad affliction of the dark dog days.

Small Changes

They are all so small, hardly there at all,
but sometimes I notice them, the changes,
and like the icy blast when a winters door
blows open, I realise that I am getter older.

We like to think we stay the same,
but like some never ending game
the changes come, little things move,
and the music of life has a different beat,
as we retreat from the main, and once again
begin to rearrange and re-evaluate,
as a less frenetic state comes to centre stage.

They are all so small, hardly there at all,
and looking back you wonder why you worried so,
for we all know that nothing lasts forever,
and we must never become blasé,
and try to say that they will.

And, as life becomes less and less organised,
and you begin to recognise that simple truth,
which you have secretly always known, -
these so small changes, these tiny rearranges,
are really just the fabric of life settling around your shoulder,
which, as you grow older, each passing day,
begins to feel more comfortable and easy.

The Sweep of a Hill

Sometimes, just the sweep of a hill, or a woodland,
still, with that first swift chill of autumn,
will give me pause, causing me to look again.
Or the smell of the fallen leaves, decaying on the ground,
or that soft, sad, particular sound the wind makes,
sighing through the almost bare branches,
and I marvel again at all the chances we take
with this world of ours.

Sometimes it's just the set of the summer sky,
the infinite blue which catches my eye,
and forces me to review such a familiar sight,
one which I have seen many times before, yet never quite like this.
And the silver flowing estuary, constant, yet ever changing,
forever rearranging it's gleaming sand bars for my delight,
and pausing again at this simple sight, I wonder anew
at all the chances we take with this world of ours.

Sometimes it's the chatter of the children on the nearby playground,
a distant, always comforting sound, familiar to me now,
and yet somehow, like the reassuring chimes of the church clock,
they are things which give me pause for thought, which set me to
wondering, how long can we go on, with no backward glances,
how long can we go on with all the fateful chances which we take with
this world of ours.

Sunday Morning Chaos

Sunday morning, and church bells chime,
the morning mist lifts from the village streets,
and begins the slow, reluctant retreat,
back up the hillside, as if loath to leave the estuary.

Early February, and light winds lift the flurry
of overnight snow, and gently blow it into neat piles
on every street corner, as it would, of course,
I think to myself, remembering the song from 'Camelot'

And I continue walking, up the steep ascent of Woodgate Hill,
where remnants of mist are lingering still within the
hollows of the land, and still I cannot really understand
just what this life of mine is all about.

But I know I'm really not cut out for philosophy,
I have enough trouble dealing with paintings, and bad poetry,
to worry too much about the meaning of life,
and yet recently I find myself questioning everything.

The good and the bad, the happy and the sad,
the whole litany of emotions which are the human condition,
I keep telling myself I'm just getting old, but truth be told,
I know it's something more than that.

And so I continue to walk the hill, the mist below me now,
but still somehow swirling around within my mind,
and I find that as I turn and head for home I'm smiling,
thinking, maybe the 'chaos theory' has something to offer!

Yearning

Days are dark, the light has gone,
and winter seems to linger on forever.
Oh how I long for summer days,
when colours change from dismal greys
to green and yellow, golden brown,
and I can feel the sun around my shoulders.

Remembered Summer II

I found the photographs yesterday,
hidden away under a pile of drawings,
both originals shot in black and white,
now turned to sepia brown,
but ageing never could put down
the beauty that shone out from them.

Her eyes, her smile, from all those years ago,
(and to this day I'll never know
just what it was she saw in me!)
but I've fallen in love all over again,
remembering her as I knew her back then,
in those so few summer days
of miracle and wonder.

An Urge to Remember, an Urge to Forget

These days my mind is always in conflict, I'm getting old,

and I only want to remember the positive aspects

of my life, but my mind is rife with other memories,

memories which I have an urge to forget, and yet,

after all these years, they haunt my memory still.

Yet things I was told only yesterday,

have already flown far away, beyond my power to recall,

and all that remains is a nagging doubt in the back of my mind,

I know that I can still recall a kaleidoscope of odd facts,

lines of poetry, whole verses, names, dates, places ,

a particular voice, a remembered face,

but other things I cannot place,

I have an urge to remember, and an urge to forget,

I just hope that I can keep them apart,

for a few more years yet . . . but I am beginning to worry.

Time

Most of the poems in this book could be put in this section,
it is a universal subject covered by most poets, and almost all poetry
touches upon it, this section in particular.

Do You Remember ?

Do you remember that summer when we were just children,-
when the school holiday seemed to last forever,
and, no matter what the weather,
we would all be outside, playing games,
for the war was almost over, but we never went away on holidays,
with six kids and only a dockers wage coming in,
our families couldn't afford such luxuries.

Do you remember the games we played
In those first post war years, without the constant fears of air raids,
Marbles, boolers, conkers in the autumn,
Cricket all through the summer, endless football and rugby,
and games of Realleo and sardines that lasted for days.
and now, remembering, I'm amazed that we got away with so much.

All the boys sneaking into Craven Park each Saturday
to watch Rovers play, getting in our favourite way,
levering up the two loose planks in the back fence,
then walking casually out from behind the stand,
Our life was grand, and we were never caught,
though now, with thought and hindsight, maybe a blind eye
was often turned in our direction!

I was a monitor in the ABC Minors at the 'Royalty' cinema,
and would smuggle all my mates in through the side door,
we did that for a whole year, watching 'Flash Gordon'
old westerns, and endless war films, most of us knew every cowboys
name, and every type of plane that flew in the war,
and all this was way before television, never mind the internet,
and yet, for most of us, it was the best time of our lives.

We never realized that most of the grown-up's knew full well
just what we were doing most of the time,
as they watched us play among the rubble and grime
of all the bombed out houses, knowing what we were doing
sneaking into the rugby and the cinema,
and just as long as we didn't go too far,
 allowing us our new found freedom,
 to run and play without the constant threat
of war.

I can hardly remember when the bombs stopped falling,
Or when we could once again sleep in our own bed,
But I remember the sun seemed to shine forever overhead.

Fathers Day

I only sent my Father one card in his entire life,
I was his eldest son, the fifth child in a family of six,
four girls and two boys, born into a house full of the noise
of young women growing up, a house where Dad would always
retreat to his shed, and his carpentry,
and he often allowed me to join him there,
a sanctuary we both could share, amid the tools and wood.
It was there that I saw the card, a picture of a man in a shed,
and under it, written in very bold red, it simply said,
'From your girls'.

I asked him what it meant, for then I was completely ignorant
of Fathers day, and when he showed me the contents,
with all the sentiments etc. I went away, a young boy,
ashamed that I had known nothing about this special day -
and determined to set things right.
I was still very young, but the next day I spent a long time drawing
a horse with a young colt by its side, galloping through a meadow,
with below, the words 'From your son'
and inside a list, thanking him for all the things which he had done
for me, - from teaching me to tie my shoelaces,
to the then more complicated mechanics of Meccano,
it was quite a long list - long enough I hoped,
to last him for the rest of his life.

Start All The Clocks

Start all the clocks, connect the telephone,
Allow the dog to chew upon the juicy bone,
Play all the pianos, and bang the big base drum,
Hang out the flags and bunting, and let all the people come.
Let aeroplanes circle soaring overhead,
Scribbling in the sky a message plainly read,
'Life is returning, never fear'
Let traffic policemen wear pink lycra gear
And in the North, the South, the East and West
We only need our Sunday rest,
So back to singing freedoms song,
I thought lockdown would last forever, I was wrong!
The stars are all wanted now. Ignite every one,
Shine up the moon and rekindle the sun,
Fill up the mighty ocean and replant all the wood.
For everything now is coming back to good.

This poem was written before the second lockdown was imposed.

With apologies to W.H.Auden.

Perhaps

Perhaps there will be more days
when they will want to sit by me
and ask for my help,
I hope that I can still be there,
that I can be allowed to share
in their quest for further knowledge.

Perhaps there will be more times
when they will seek my company,
when they will turn to me
and want to share my experiences,
I hope that I can still be there,
to help and encourage them
to try their new ideas out.

Perhaps there will be more years
for us to be together,
but whatever the future holds,
I hope that I can still be there,
can still be allowed to share, if only in memory,
and when they think of me
I hope, perhaps, it is with love
and affection.

Old Lines

They call out to me from the old church yard,
The rows of headstones standing guard,
Over those who will never run away.
Some stand aslant through lack of care,
Inscriptions so worn they are scarcely there,
And yet they move me so.
The sorrow and tragedy plainly there to see,
Deeply etched into each headstone,
Hinting at lives and times unknown.

The distraught parents, the child only seven,
The eroded inscription, 'Lord, keep him in heaven,
Until we get there'
The grave, dated 1898, of little Jonathan,
Well beloved, and only son, of Mary and Jonathan Ross,
And you wonder how they ever lived with such a loss,
The terrible cross they bore for so long,
And as you leave you offer a silent prayer,
That he was still there,- and waiting for them.

Detritus

Clear, cloudless, winter pale sky,
and I, out there alone on the top of the hill,
standing stock still under it's awesome immensity.
To my left the quarry is stark and white,
almost luminous against such light,
and to my right proud Swanland sits,
prim and proper, as befits it's position
within the local hierarchy,
whilst down the hill North Ferriby
sits snug and warm against the rivers edge.

And standing alone amid this sky and space,
I begin to realise our true place
within the scheme of it's immensity,
and I wonder once again why we
should deem to think we know so much,
for in reality we're just the dust, the detritus,
that causes not one blink in God's impassive eye.

Quantum Leap

We live on a very small planet,
sitting in a very small constellation,
within a huge and ever expanding universe -
Yet we have developed language,
we are able to converse, we are, almost, civilized,
we can think of abstract ideas, like our leap years,
in order to make the mathematics and synchronization
of our calendar and solar years live in harmony with one another,
and there are many, many other things which the human race
has achieved, which seem to me like miracles.
We have harnessed the Sun's rays,
we have made the Quantum leap into space,
and soon, in some distant year of peace and grace
we will be able to keep our contract with our true destiny,
and make another Quantum leap, a leap of faith and hope
as we reach out to other galaxies and other intelligent entities,
for there must surely be many.
It will be the final Quantum leap, which you and me will not be there
to see, but our children's, children's, children just might be there to
take that final Quantum leap...and against all odds,
watch as mankind become as Gods.

Punk Poet.(Now't to say)

He reads the words fast, like they may never last,
spitting them out in a crescendo of sound,
and like bullets they flash and fly around,
and you have to concentrate on each word, every line,
every movement, every jump, every threatening sign,
for he jerks and he jumps around all the time,
shaking his fists when his words sometimes rhyme,
he challenges you with every word that he shouts,
'cos he's secretly worried that his words mean now't,
but he's just a working class poet, poor bloke,
and he just loves to have a good poke,
- at the old establishment!

So he screams and he swears, and waves his arms about,
and keeps repeating lines that are really saying now't !
but he's a working class punk poet, and one of the boys,
and he really thinks that if he makes one helluva noise,
and jerks and jumps, giving it plenty of hype,
that people won't notice that his words are all tripe !
He still wears his hair long, although he's going bald,
and you suddenly realize that he's getting a bit old,
with his sad zoot suits from the sixties, and his wispy grey
moustache,
he looks like an eccentric, with not quite enough cash,
but he's a working class punk poet, and one of the boys,
and though he still swears and curses, there's never quite so much
noise,
for his words now lack the venom, and his verses still don't rhyme,
and the fading punk poet knows that he is now well past his prime -
and secretly he's thinking about joining, - the old establishment!

Alone in a Crowd

It would be so much better if seven o'clock
came a little bit later in the day,
allowing me a little more time to put my dreams away,
and silently ease myself back into life's brittle reality,
but no ! - there can be no such luxury for me . . .
time to get up and get showered, get shaved, get dressed,
watching, as from the shaving mirror my fathers face looks out,
his eyes reflecting all my worry, my raging doubt,
for though he died much younger than I will ever now be,
I can only ever remember him as being so much older than me,
and I wonder again how much longer I will manage to last,
with less time in my future than I have in my past,

And throughout another busy but uneventful day
 I successfully hide all my doubts away,
I put on a show, smiling and talking to people,
feigning interest, whilst getting on with what's left of my life,
I have no pressing need for recognition, fame, or wealth,
and my fears and my doubts I keep to myself,
as I watch for signs in other people of my age,
and secretly speculate, if they too all rage against the dying of the
light,
as they all pass through my line of thought and sight,
each one alone . . . alone like me . . . alone in a crowd.

Tanks for a memory

By WILL BENNETT

ONE CHARLIE, the tank that played a vital role in the Second World War, has been restored to its former glory with the help of The Mail on Sunday.

The Churchill engineers assault tank has remained on the beach at Graye-sur-Mer in Normandy since the D-Day invasion in 1944.

There, stuck in a crater, it was used by the 26 Assault Squadron Royal Engineers to support a bridge, enabling the Allies to pour off the beach-head.

Sappers from the present 26 Squadron (left) worked for three weeks to renovate

One Charlie on the very spot where their predecessors fought and died. Now the tank will serve as a' fitting memorial.

Last week Major General Tony Younger, who commanded the squadron on D-Day, and two other veterans, ex-Sergeant Harold Fielder and ex-Corporal Ronald Cross, attended a ceremony to mark the restoration (below left).

The project was financed by contributions from British industry and The Mail on Sunday, and the sappers were put up by local villagers.

Pictures: LYNN HILTON

The article 'Tanks for a memory' appeared in 'The Mail on Sunday' on 27th March 1988. The memorial is at Graye-sur-Mer, Normandy.

One Charlie

As soon as I opened the paper that day
the picture jumped out at me,
stunning in its familiarity and content,
for there they were, a group of soldiers,
in overalls, their berets tipped forward rakishly,
(tankies, we called ourselves, with a kind of inverted
snobbery, for we were really Royal Engineers),
all crouched down in the familiar pose,
in front of the giant machine, which rose
like a mechanical dinosaur from behind them.
'Tanks for a memory' the headline read,
and in the article beneath it said,
"Sappers from the present 26 Assault squadron"
and suddenly all the memories came flooding back,
and once again I was with them, riding the track.

We were such a small unit even back then,
four crew of three tanks, just twelve in all,
and constantly seeming to be on call
by the so called 'elite' of the division,
the third and fourth tanks, in their thundering cents,
and the lancers, who were, as always, hell bent
on 'death or glory'.
The gunners, the drivers, the radio men,
the call signs, 'One Alpha, One Bravo, One Charlie'
and then, 'hear netting call - nett now'
and remembering the faces I started wondering
just how many of my troop were just sitting, like me,
and recalling the memories of what used to be.

It all seems now like another age,
just a picture and article there on the page,
a memory of times long gone by, and yet,
I know that somehow I will never forget,
One Alpha, One Bravo, and One Charlie,
and the 'tankies' who shared
all those hard times with me.

Retrospective

Albinoni escapes from the radio in a slow
somehow mournful adagio, the light is fading,
and out through the window squares of light appear,
I feel somehow unsettled, restless,
as if time is escaping from me.

I hear the music without really listening,
allowing it to seep into my unconsciousness,
my mind slipping into the mood of the gathering gloom,
as the late October afternoon ebbs away into the evening,
I feel a sadness I cannot explain.

A melancholy, empty pain, as if the whole world were sighing,
and yet I have no reason for sorrow, for I have all I need
to make tomorrow the same as my today,
a mirror of all my yesterdays, whose serried ranks
all fade away into the distant past.

And maybe, I think, in some strange and convoluted way,
this is the cause of my sadness, for I feel somehow unsettled,
as if life is closing down on me, narrowing my options
until I am not what I would want to be,
and I rise, stirring restlessly, like a caged animal.

But then, pulling the curtains together I shut out
the world outside, and settling back in front of the typewriter
I reach out and change the tape, smiling to myself
as Simon and Garfunkel fill the room
with soft memories of the sixties,
and I begin to consider the next line.

Nature

Here is unfenced existence:
Facing the sun, untalkative, out of reach.

Philip Larkin

Hull's hazily utopian green,
Reaching out across nocturnal Holderness.

Douglas Dunn

The Earth Turns

The colours are changing, beckoning the practiced eye,
as slanted light fills up the vaulted sky
with strokes of wonderment and colour,
sweeping the canvassed surface with movement,
the brush now never still, it's line commanding leaf and limb,
and within the painters eye the mist makes
ghostly dim, the landscape . . .

and the earth turns . . .

Colours change as green gives way to gold and brown,
and deeper down, the mind commands the eye,
and earth and sky become the artists artifacts.
The light is changing, moving, still,
cloud shadow patterns climb the hill,
paint changing shape and substance
as ideas advance . . .

And the earth turns . . .

Patterns emerge, and shapes recede,
the ever changing need to capture mood and content,
and throughout it all that deep intent
within each artists mind, to paint and paint,
each stroke, each scratch, each scrape,
with hand and eye and mind, to look,
to find, and to create . . .

And the earth turns . . .

Autumn Song

And now the branches stand cold and bare,
for the leaves are beginning to fall,
and the wind is sighing that soft, slow song
who's title I cannot recall.

And the lane is a carpet of colours
which the wind will constantly change,
and the lines of the song run on through my mind
as my heart seeks to re-arrange.

For the land around me is now closing down
as the first frosts of winter appear,
and I feel that old song beginning to fade,
now that you will no longer be here.

I fear you are gone to a place far away,
as the leaves flutter soft to the ground,
and I feel the first chill of emptiness,
as deep winter circles around.

The Sweep of a Hill

Sometimes, just the sweep of a hill, or a woodland,
still, with that first swift chill of autumn,
will give me pause, causing me to look again.
Or the smell of the fallen leaves, decaying on the ground,
or that soft, sad, particular sound the wind makes,
sighing through the almost bare branches,
and I marvel again at all the chances we take
with this world of ours.

Sometimes it's just the set of the summer sky,
the infinite blue which catches my eye,
and forces me to review such a familiar sight,
one which I have seen many times before, yet never quite like this.
And the silver flowing estuary, constant, yet ever changing,
forever rearranging it's gleaming sand bars for my delight,
and pausing again at this simple sight, I wonder anew
at all the chances we take with this world of ours.

Sometimes it's the chatter of the children on the nearby playground,
a distant, always comforting sound, familiar to me now,
and yet somehow, like the reassuring chimes of the church clock,
they are things which give me pause for thought, which set me to
wondering, how long can we go on, with no backward glances,
how long can we go on with all the fateful chances which we take with
this world of ours.

The Woods in Autum

Red and yellow, and golden brown,
the autumn leaves come drifting down,
and all around, the ground becomes
a kaleidoscope of colour, unlike any other,
a swirling, ever changing drift of the
bright shades of autumn.
I feel an empathy with these woods, these trees,
I know their every mood, I feel each different breeze,
I am at home on their paths, with their different horizons.
I have watched as they celebrate the joy of each spring,
the fullness of summer, the bitterness of winter's cold,
and always that mixture of joy and sadness which
will be forever my memory of these woods in autumn.

For I remember our young love, and that old sweet song,
the crunching of the leaves as we walked along,
 through the woods on those hazy autumn days,
the colours which still forever amaze,
the wind stirring memories of the way that we were,
and the comfort of knowing that you will be there,
when I return again from these autumn woods.

Sunday Morning Chaos

Sunday morning, and church bells chime,
the morning mist lifts from the village streets,
and begins the slow, reluctant retreat,
back up the hillside, as if loath to leave the estuary.

Early February, and light winds lift the flurry
of overnight snow, and gently blow it into neat piles
on every street corner, as it would, of course,
I think to myself, remembering the song from 'Camelot'

And I continue walking, up the steep ascent of Woodgate Hill,
where remnants of mist are lingering still within the
hollows of the land, and still I cannot really understand
just what this life of mine is all about.

But I know I'm really not cut out for philosophy,
I have enough trouble dealing with paintings, and bad poetry,
to worry too much about the meaning of life,
and yet recently I find myself questioning everything.

The good and the bad, the happy and the sad,
the whole litany of emotions which are the human condition,
I keep telling myself I'm just getting old, but truth be told,
I know it's something more than that.

And so I continue to walk the hill, the mist below me now,
but still somehow swirling around within my mind,
and I find that as I turn and head for home I'm smiling,
thinking, maybe the 'chaos theory' has something to offer!

Winterwood

In winterwood the trees stand bare,
there is soft silence everywhere,
no crackle of footsteps on the frozen ground,
and nowhere any semblance of sound,
no wind sighs through the naked trees,
no rustle of leaves, no whispering breeze,
and all around, the air is tinged with expectation.

I have been here many times before,
sketching these trees in every season, I saw,
the first surge of their spring awakening,
and the fullness of the summer foliage,
then the sweet sad joy of autumn's colours, and,
as now, locked in winter's iron hand, which turns the land,
into a subtle monochrome of spectral images.

I sketch quickly, before my hands become too cold,
such that I can no longer hold my pencil steady,
and later, as I leave, I know already that I will return,
for winterwood will always give me much to learn,
and as I study the contours of the trees, the lie of the land,
I try again to understand, the magic that is Winterwood,
for I know that I should, with so few years left to me now.

Sometimes

Sometimes in late September, when the nights start drawing in,
and that special autumn light begins to fill up the evening sky,
I start to dream of days gone by, of days which now are sepia brown,
old photographs of memories which are pasted down
to black pages in an album, or in a faded yellow folder which,
as we grow older, become, each one, so much
like pieces of a stained glass window.

Sometimes, deep in the cutting cold of a December day,
when summer seems so far away I begin to think it never happened,
and Christmas is still like a tinsel dream, somehow unreal,
dressing up the big stores windows, sometimes I can hear a tune
on the radio, something I whistled a long time ago,
and almost as though it were yesterday the images come
flooding back and I am warmed by their memory.

Sometimes when spring is only a thought away,
and the trees have that green haze of budding,
when the rain has stopped, and the sun is testing itself out,
throwing latticed shadows through the still bare branches,
sometimes I wonder at all the chances we take,
and all the mistakes we all make, as our lives roll onward.

And sometimes, in the stillness of a summer day,
with light patterns dancing in a red haze under my
heat closed eyes, I feel the cloudless sky's immensity,
and wonder once again, why me? Why should I always
feel so much, its so unjust,~ but then I listen to other things,
a line remembered which always brings me back,
back down to reality, and I know that I can see,
can reach out and touch the hand, can understand,
can meet the eye, can say I love you, and watch the sky
fill up with wonder, as the great flag of happiness unfurls.

Spring Equinox

The light is changing, and spring is busy,
rearranging the garden, and the fields,
and the river, the light and the shade,
the movement and the still,
and I can feel the dark earth fill
and start to swell with pregnant pride,
like a woman heavy with child.

The height of the sky increases,
cloud patterns change, and infinite blue
begins to range across the void.
Lawnmowers awake from their winter hibernation,
and all across this sun starved nation
people emerge into the first day of clear
Crystalline air, aware that there is always
one day when the light starts changing,
when suddenly spring is here, rearranging.

Going to Little Switzerland

We rode the path by the river side,
following the oily, ebbing tide,
just Joe and me, our tyres
crunching over the loose shale,
the sunshine pale, gleaming dull on the water,
going to Little Switzerland.

Just Joe and me, talking and
singing a nonsense song as we
rode along, oblivious to everything
except ourselves, our bikes, and the glorious day,
and the buddleia butterflies which got in our way,
going to Little Switzerland.

Just Joe and me on that short afternoon,
and a magical time which was over too soon,
but a memory to keep for as long as I live,
one which I know will always give,
that secret surge of pleasure,
whenever I think of Joe and me,
going to Little Switzerland.

'Little Switzerland' is the local name for an old disused quarry, now
full of trees, tracks, and little lakes which contain newts and tiddlers.

Deep Winter

And now the branches stand cold and bare,
for the leaves are beginning to fall,
and the wind is sighing that soft, slow song,
who's title I cannot recall.

And the lane is a carpet of colours,
which the wind will constantly change,
and the lines of the song run on through my mind
as my heart seeks to re-arrange.

For the land around me is closing down
as the first frosts of winter appear,
and I feel that my heart is turning to stone,
now that you can no longer be near.

For you are now gone to a place far away
A place that can never be found,
and I feel the first chill of emptiness,
as deep winter circles around.

Ageing

(Rage, Rage, against the dying of the light)

This section of the book is about ageing, - something we all do,

all at the same pace, something we cannot control,

and for most of our lives pay little attention to, only when the big

birthdays come do we begin to worry...

A Day in the Life

It would be so much better if seven o'clock
came a little bit later in the day,
allowing me more time to put my dreams away,
and ease myself back into reality.
Time to get up, get shaved, get showered, get dressed,
whilst I watch the world in all its sad distress
as I ingest the morning news along with my toast and cereal.

Whilst once again wondering, as I always seem to do now,
just how much longer I will manage to last,
with less time in the future than I have in the past.
And in the shaving mirror my fathers face looks out,
his eyes reflecting my apprehension and doubt,
and though he died much younger than I'll ever now be,
I always think of him, somehow, as so much older than me.

And all through another easy, and uneventful day,
I successfully hide all my doubts away,
and I smile, for I know that I'll never be famous, or wealthy
I just think myself lucky that I'm still here, and still healthy,
and yet still I watch closely other people my age,
and idly speculate, do they secretly rage, and rage,
against the dying of the light.

Only One Dread

I have no dread of each passing year,
and as I age I feel no encroaching fear
for whatever it is that lies ahead, - instead,
I look forward to becoming a proper 'old man'
someone who can do whatever he wants to do,
swear like a trooper 'til the air turns blue,
paint pictures that don't mean anything at all,
and will never see the Feren's hallowed wall.

Write poetry, with an increasingly trembling hand,
full of themes and ideas which only I understand,
and for light relief, some bawdy comic verse,
full of Mabels and Beryls, and often much worse,
but just like all poets and proper old men,
I won't worry what words drip from the nib of my pen.

But as I get older I have only one dread,
one dread which I cannot get out of my head,
forget my sex life, - now long gone,
forget my knees with the cartilage worn,
forget all the games which I used to play,
for I always knew there would come a day
when I became too old for all that.

The only thing which I hold in fear,
is the terrible thought that maybe one year,
when I am creaky old, and in a bit of a haze,
that I may be made to spend my last days,
behind tightly closed curtains on Retirement row,
Oh Lord, please save me from the bloody beige
bungalow !

Blessed

It happened outside of Sainsbury's, as I returned my empty trolley
to the rack.

I saw the old man standing there alone, looking forlorn and vaguely
bewildered as he patted his pockets, and stared around,
his eyes seeming to show a lack of comprehension.

"Are you alright Sir?" I asked, as I collected my pound coin from the
trolley, "Do you need any help?" And he looked at me then,
his eyes still vague and far away, "It's my change you see" he said,
pointing to the trolleys, "I've left it all at home"
and he slowly shook his head.

I looked at him again then, standing there so forlorn, so bewildered,
so lost, and reaching out I took his hand and placed my coin in it,
"Have this one on me" I said, "and have yourself a Merry Christmas"
And as I turned to walk away I heard the old man softly say,
"May God bless you Sir" - and for that brief moment I really did feel
as if I had been blessed.

Black Dog

The black dog comes to me more often now,
always sniffing round, sowing the seeds of all
our discontent.
As if hell bent on tearing us apart,
he snaps and snarls within my heart,
and I cannot live with his growing rage,
cannot engage, for there is never common ground,
for I know whenever he's around,
all reason leaves the room.

It never used to be this way, we had our differences, it's true,
you would often blame me, and I would always blame you,
and we would turn them into arguments, which made no sense,
but, though intense, would soon blow over,
Like a storm cloud on a summers day,
but then the black dog invaded my head, and though nothing was said,
nothing was ever quite the same.

I age,(and feel the change, as all men do)
not into something bold and new,
but something old, and cold, and different.
Something I know which black dog prays upon,
attacking where our youth has gone,
those soft and tender places in our two close
linked memories, as we both seize
on each mistake, which even now we both still make,
and as the bones of discontentment break,
I feel my life disintegrate...
                        ... and fall scattered all around.

Changes

I feel, increasingly, as if I'm getting it wrong,

as if, somehow, I don't belong in this modern world.

"Chill out Dad" my daughter says,

"language changes, we don't always use your words now"

and though I know she's right, I still wonder how it all came to this.

Increasingly, I am aware of subtle shifts of authority,

tectonic plates of opinion move around me, and I am left in isolation,

my sense of natural right usurped by media manipulation

until all feeling of justice is gone.I search for points of reference,

indications of what is now considered correct,

but, I suspect, that now I would not recognize them -

common sense, manners, a sense of right and wrong,

within the young, they are all gone. - or so it seems,

and only yesterday's dreams remind me

of our once brave new world.

Losing Her

We were both too stubborn to stop,
to give in, too proud to let the other win,
a trivial argument about nothing at all,
which has left us both in pain, and once again
I feel that I am losing her.

These days we seem to argue more,
it's almost as if we have a score to settle,
both forever on our mettle, and it's so hard
when afterwards she walks away without a word,
and again I fear that I am losing her.

And yet we still agree on so many things,
and I know that whatever hardship this life brings,
she will always be on my side, and I on hers,
I know, and she knows too, that we both of us care,
yet still, sometimes, somehow, I feel that I am losing her.

I'm a proud and stubborn old man,
and she is a proud and stubborn young lady,
but maybe, just maybe, we can work it out,
for love and affection are always there,
and no father ever loved his daughter
as much as I love her.

The Weight of Age

I feel the weight of age across my shoulders,

sitting like so many heavy boulders,

a lifetime's collection of rights and wrongs

within my mind, and I can never seem to find

the consolation of forgiveness.

No shining whites, no darkest black,

and yet, with hindsight, looking back,

I can see only various shades of grey,

spread over the palette of my life,

as if all the effort, all the strife,

meant nothing at all, and all that I ever can recall

is the comfort of conformity.

As we age we all want to leave our mark,

to ensure the arc of our achievements are recorded,

if only for the children that come after us,

yet as I grow older I realise, though not with any real surprise,

that my only legacy will be my love for them, - my family.

The Good Old Days

Memory escapes us, shapes us,

plays tricks on us like a childhood friend.

Filters our view of to-days circumstances

through the lens of past events.

Lessons we have learned,

stories we can recite the endings to.

even our most clever, original thoughts

are often only shiny stones gathered from

the riverbed of our past.

Memory moulds us, holds us,

makes us aware of what is

important in life.

a family story, a golden oldie,

a tried and true, and just like me, or you

we didn't really do the pally glide,

or play all day on the old park slide,

or any of the false memories of a misspent youth.

and yet we claim the grandest prize,- in many ways,-

our memories of the 'good old days'

Not a Young Mans Death

He's such a toff, that Roger McGough,
that he writes all his words in rhyme,
and it just goes to show, that you never quite know,
where you will end up, in time.
For when he was young and still wet round the ears,
he'd go down to the clubs and have a few beers,
he wrote songs for 'The scaffold' - like 'Lily the pink'
and he ran with the Beatles,- or so people think.
He lived by the slogan(which he nicked from James Dean)
'Live fast – die young' – for life was just a dream.

But he didn't die young, - and now never lives fast,
now his 'young man's death' is just a ghost from the past,
for he's now pushing eighty, - the same age as me,
and I know just how depressing all that lot can be,
now he lives in London, and wears proper shirts AND ties,
he's in demand for lectures, readings, and other arty lies,
he has just published another book of his poetry,
and entitled it just 'Eighty' - with oh such awesome wit,
and if you do nothing more, and are in need of a smile,
try reading his minds wonderings for just a little while,
for inside there is a poem, called, with tongue in cheek,
'not for me a young mans death'- with all the humour you could seek,
Which, I think, just about sums it all up!

Roger old son, I salute you!

Reading Titles

It is something which I often do,

whilst sitting in my studio (the third bedroom, in another life)

with Spotify playing from my list of music,

I register the favourite bits - lines from the songs

which are playing, or titles from the books

which fill the shelves in front of me,

titles which I know will be

all too familiar within my mind, and I find

myself remembering the stories they told,

or the information they hold, the pictures, the references,

and all the knowledge - and I silently pledge to read more,

although I already feel that I know the final score -

for my eyesight is slowly failing, and like most old men

I can now only read for limited periods of time,

and like a poem which doesn't always seem to rhyme,

I find this failing upsets my reading pleasure.

The old age influence is creeping in around me,

limiting my options, surprising me,

and causing me to begin to doubt my own abilities.

But then I reconsider, I can still write, I can still paint and draw,

And what is more, I still sing in the choir, I'm eighty three, not ninety four,

And no more will I let this bloody plague of old age influence me.